Foreword

My Dad Loves Me, My Dad Has A Disease was originally written as a result of my work with young people who had a parent in treatment for their alcoholism. These children were learning at a very young age that it was not safe for them to openly talk about their family experiences. Art therapy was a wonderful medium for them to find the words and a voice in which to talk honestly. It was also a wonderful tool in which to not only share feelings but to problem solve, lessen denial, and to put words to that which was so confusing.

The original pictures were all drawn and the stories written by children ages five through fourteen that had one or two alcoholic parents. After many years and thousands of children using this workbook, My Dad Loves Me, My Dad Has A Disease has been revised to address the fact that today, if a child lives with addiction, it may not be alcohol addiction. The family member may be addicted to other drugs as well. Words have been rewritten, some pictures changed and new pictures added making it possible for more children of addiction to experience their own recovery process.

The basic premise of this book is that chemical dependency is a disease — the alcoholic/addict is a sick person not a bad person. This disease affects not only the addicted person but those who love that person as well. This is a book that will help the "others" affected by chemical dependency to become well.

Claudia Black, Ph.D., MSW
Author

MAC Publishing, Bainbridge Island, Washington, 98110 • (206) 842-6303 • (800) 698-0148 •

www.claudiablack.com

Dedicated to

Tammy Lynn Stark, a dear friend and wonderful soul.

Acknowledgments

Special Thanks to:

The many children who shared their experiences and trust through their stories and illustrations!

Tommy Mimikos, as a consultant for his extra effort!

The numerous people who have supported and encouraged me in my work with the children, especially, Don Steckdaub, Lucille Sidenberg, Anne Elkin, Jack Rose, Deborah Parker and Victoria Danzig.

Barbara Hopkins, who was directly involved in much of my work with the children.

My mother Lee Gilmore, my sister Jana Kay, and my grandmother Mary Margaret Foss Dolquist; I know it has caused us to relive old feelings.

NACOA — Several years have passed since the first printing and first edition of this book. During that time the National Association for Children of Alcoholics (NACOA) has been created. I want to thank every member, board member, advisory board member, staff and volunteer for the difference you have made in hundreds of thousands of children's lives.

And Jack F., this book is for us and the thousands of children like us growing up in addicted homes.

Table of Contents

Chapter 1
ADDICTION

When your mom, dad, grandparent, or anyone close to you becomes addicted to alcohol or other drugs, it not only hurts them, it hurts those who love them too.

Alcohol and drugs are like dominoes. They knock down the person who knocks down everyone including themselves.

The alcoholic/addict is not a bad or mean person, but is an injured person. They are sick; they have a disease called addiction.

Paper sticks to glue.
Magnets stick to metal.
Bees stick to flowers.

An alcoholic/addict is stuck to alcohol and/or other drugs, such as marijuana, cocaine, heroin, crystal meth (amphetamines), or possibly prescription pills. There is a word for "being stuck;" the word is addicted. It means to have a habit that is very, very hard to break. Draw a picture of what you think addiction looks like.

My Bee is stuck to the flower

And can't get off.

like an alcoholic is stuck to alchol

Once he starts, he **CAN'T** stop.

CAN'T STOP— It's hard to imagine anything that you can't stop, but it's true for someone who has become addicted to alcohol or other drugs. They are people who need to learn to not drink or use at all because once they are drinking or using, they find they don't have the ability to stop — they keep going back for more.

when my dad drinks he is two
different people when he's been drinking

I don't know which Mom I'll be coming home to.

When an alcoholic/addict drinks or uses, they change a lot.
Sometimes it seems like they become different people, and that's very confusing.
Does the alcoholic/addict in your life change when they drink or use?
Draw a picture about it.

We know that many times a person who drinks or uses acts like two different people. But sometimes the other parent — the one who isn't addicted — also acts like a different person. They get so concerned about the drinking and using, and feel so bad, they often misdirect their hurt feelings and treat the kids in ways they don't mean.

14

My Mother hides Her Drinks

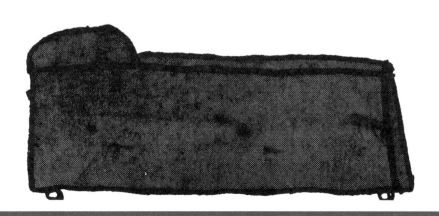

(But she doesn't hide them very well.)

Sometimes people who are addicted do things that seem very silly, like hiding their bottles or pills. This is another thing that is really hard to understand. Remember, they are sick. This is why they act different and sometimes do things that seem foolish; it's part of the disease.

Once I was Playing hide n' Seek, when my dad Came "in the room where I was hiding. He Pulled a bottle out From where I was hiding, he saw me hiding, but he didn't say anything I didn't say anything either.

Does your Mom or Dad hide their bottles, pills or other drugs?
Draw a picture of where they hide them.

Sometimes he denies things he knew he did.

DENIAL— When you pretend that something didn't really happen, it's called denial. It's almost like telling yourself a lie. Sometimes addicted parents pretend that bad things didn't happen when they were drinking or using. They just push the bad things out of their mind. We often feel bad when these things happen, we deny how we really feel, too.

When my mom drinks I just pretend she doesnt. I never even talk about it.

Draw a picture about something you want to forget,
something you want to pretend never really happened.

My Dad does drugs, but he won't admit it. That makes my mom really mad and they fight about it a lot.

Everyone in an addicted family learns to deny, such as

Dad   denies that mom has a drug problem.
              denies he has a drinking problem.
              pretends he is sick with the flu when he really has a hangover.

Mom   denies that her bruise came from her falling when she was loaded.
              says she stumbled trying to answer the phone.
              denies she was crying, but I saw her.

I   deny. I say I am not embarrassed, but I am.
              pretend I didn't hear the arguing, but I did.
              act like everything is okay, but it isn't.

Now you can fill in the blank about when you or other people in your family deny or pretend it is different than it really is.

Dad   _____ .

_____ .

_____ .

Mom   _____ .

_____ .

_____ .

Me   _____ .

_____ .

_____ .

Sister   _____ .

_____ .

_____ .

Brother   _____ .

_____ .

_____ .

BLACKOUTS — Sometimes alcoholics/addicts have blackouts. That means that they say and do things that they can't remember. They don't remember because the drug affects the brain, and the brain controls memory. When they have blackouts, they are awake and act like they know where they are and what they are saying, but later on they don't remember anything that happened.

Do you think your Mom or Dad has had a blackout?
Draw a picture about it.

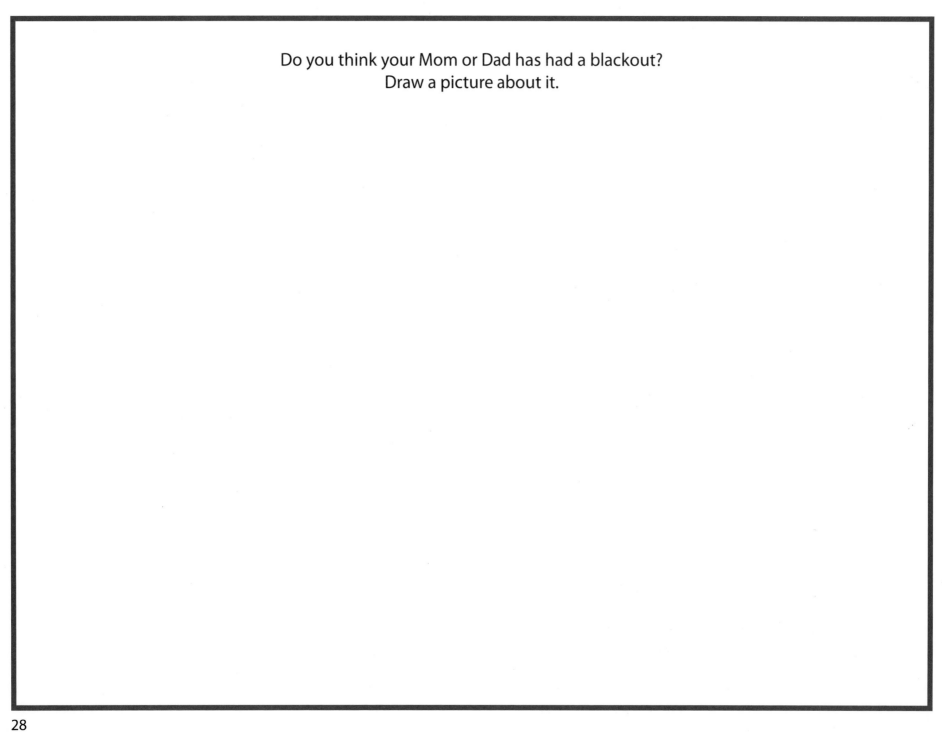

Black outs are scary! And may cost your friendship.

Getting blamed for something I did not do.

This happens in everybody's home at times
but happens more often in an addictive home.

Do you ever get blamed for something you did not do?
Draw a picture or write a story about it.

Some things to think about . . .

☆ Chemically dependent people are sick; they have a disease called addiction.

☆ Once they take the first drink or drug, they can't stop drinking or using.

☆ If your Mom or Dad is addicted, you will probably see them act "different" when they drink or use. Sometimes they may do things that seem silly, other times they do things that are scary, confusing and maybe just strange.

☆ Often times the alcoholic/addict will deny their drinking or using, and others around them will deny their feelings about them.

☆ Sometimes the alcoholic can't remember what he said or did because of a blackout.

☆ Alcoholics/addicts don't mean to act like they do, alcohol or the drug has control over them.

Chapter 2

OUR FEELINGS

I FEEL scared when my mother drinks.

Do You Ever Feel?

- Loved
- Afraid
- Warm
- Worried
- Caring
- Sad
- Patient
- Confused
- Scared
- Important
- Violent
- Angry
- Special
- Hurt
- Strong
- Embarrassed
- Jealous
- Understanding

- Ashamed
- Frightened
- Happy
- Shy
- Excited
- Understood
- Mixed-up
- Good
- Guilty
- Mean
- Comfortable
- Loving
- Upset
- Sympathetic
- Moody
- Discouraged
- Silly
- Nice

- Frustrated
- Brave
- Awful
- Curious
- Sensitive
- Terrible
- Mad
- Funny
- Daring
- Wonderful
- Gloomy
- Encouraged
- Hateful
- Uncomfortable
- Bad
- Different

When my mother does drugs I worry, I want a hug, and I feel sad. When my mom doesn't do drugs I feel warm, but I am still afraid, and still worried.

I FEEL Scared when my mother drinks.

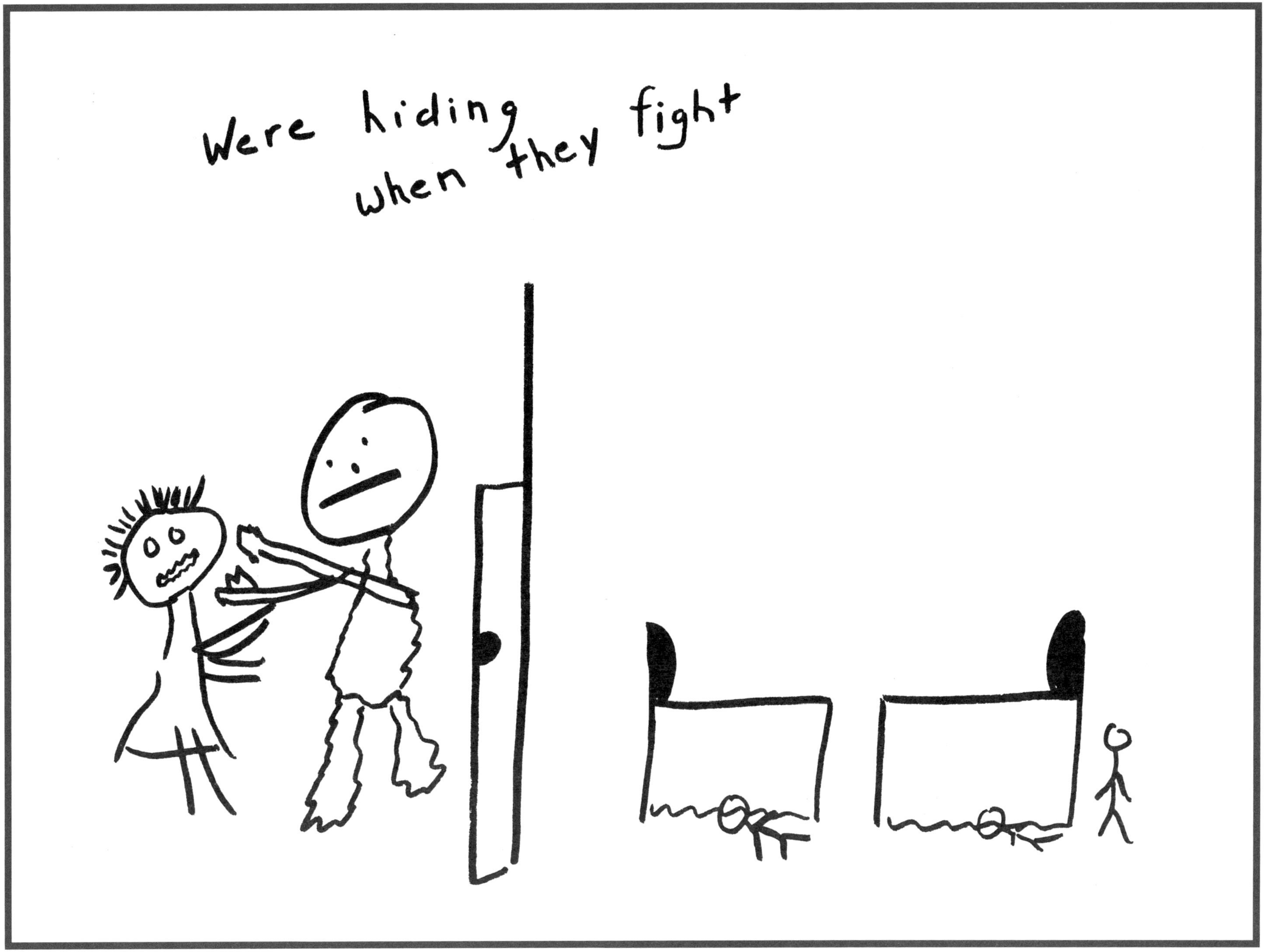
Were hiding when they fight

Do you ever get scared?
Draw a picture.

38

My Dad takes all the money for his drugs...

so we never get anything like bikes.

Show what you do when you feel mad.

42

Sometimes parents do things that disappoint and embarrass their kids.
It is often hard to tell people about those times but if you can write a story
or draw a picture, it may then be easier to talk about the problem.

Draw a picture of how you feel about the alcohol or other drug
when your parent is drinking or using.

Alcoholics/addicts sometimes become very angry and try to hurt those they love the most.
Sometimes the family members become violent and try to hurt the alcoholic/addict.
Other times family members try to hurt each other or maybe the family pet.
This doesn't happen in all families but it does in some. Have you ever been
hurt or watched someone else in your family get hurt?
Draw a picture about how you felt.

Violence come's with the Alcohol.
I'll smack you any time I want
oh know you won't.
I'm scared.

I feel guilty, I think I made her drink because I was a bad kid. Kind of like if I would have been good then she would've not drank.

We often feel it is our fault when our parent drinks or uses drugs. It is very important to know that it is not our fault. Sometimes alcoholics/addicts blame other people for their drinking and using, but other people do not make them drink or use. They would drink or use even if we were good all of the time.

I got mad at her drinking but I didn't tell her because I thought she would drink more.

Do you ever feel guilty because you think something you did or said
caused your Mom or Dad to drink or use drugs?
Draw a picture showing what happened.

my mother Love's me deep down buT. Some Time's I Think she doe's not Love me.

When our parents are addicted we sometimes get confused about how they feel about us and how we feel about them. Usually our Mom and Dad are nice to us, but often when they are drinking or using, they aren't nice anymore. Sometimes what our parents do when they are drinking or using expresses exactly the opposite of what they really feel. Alcohol and other drugs make them act differently.

At times when our parents drink or use, we aren't sure if we love them at all. We may even hate them during those times; we may think that hate is the only feeling we have. Really, both feelings are true, love and hate. At a certain moment, we may have only one strong feeling, hate, but that's only for that particular moment. All the other feelings, like love, are still inside of us, and they come back very quickly.

Love is caring enough to Help But Sometimes it runs out.

PATIENCE

I have to have patience
when my mom drinks.

The person really Isn't bad,
The person is really good. inside

Sometimes we don't like the way our Mom or Dad act. We usually know that they are really good on the inside. How do you feel about your parents? Draw a picture. How do you feel about yourself? Draw a picture.

Some things to think about . . .

☆ It's normal and natural to have feelings. People all over the world sometimes feel angry, or frightened, or loving, plus a great many more feelings.

☆ Everyone gets confused and mixed-up about their feelings. Sometimes people feel ashamed of their feelings, and they try to keep them a secret.

☆ Sometimes people push away their feelings and don't let them come into their mind, but feelings have to go somewhere. Feelings that have nowhere to go become headaches, or stomachaches, or make us feel dizzy, or very tired.

☆ We learn about our feelings by listening quietly to them, by talking about them with others, and by writing and drawing pictures about them.

☆ Sometimes we just need to let our feelings happen and accept them, so we can understand them.

Chapter 3

GETTING WELL

"My dad Feels better and I'm FeEling the Same way.

My dad always got drunk before, now he comes here and he doesn't get drunk any more. Before I always got mad at him for getting drunk, but now I don't because he doesn't get drunk, I'm glad.

It's a sickness that goes on inside of you. But if you really want to stop, you can. You have to ask for help.

When alcoholics/addicts want to stop drinking or using, they ask other people for help. Some ask for help by going to a treatment program or hospital; others ask for help by going to meetings called AA (Alcoholics Anonymous) or NA (Narcotics Anonymous) or CA (Cocaine Anonymous). Some people do a combination of both, a treatment program and meetings.

Has your parent asked for help to stop drinking or using? Draw a picture about it.

A.A is a group of people trying to help themseles and other people by giving their experiekes of what it was like wene they drank and how happy they are now that they are Sober.

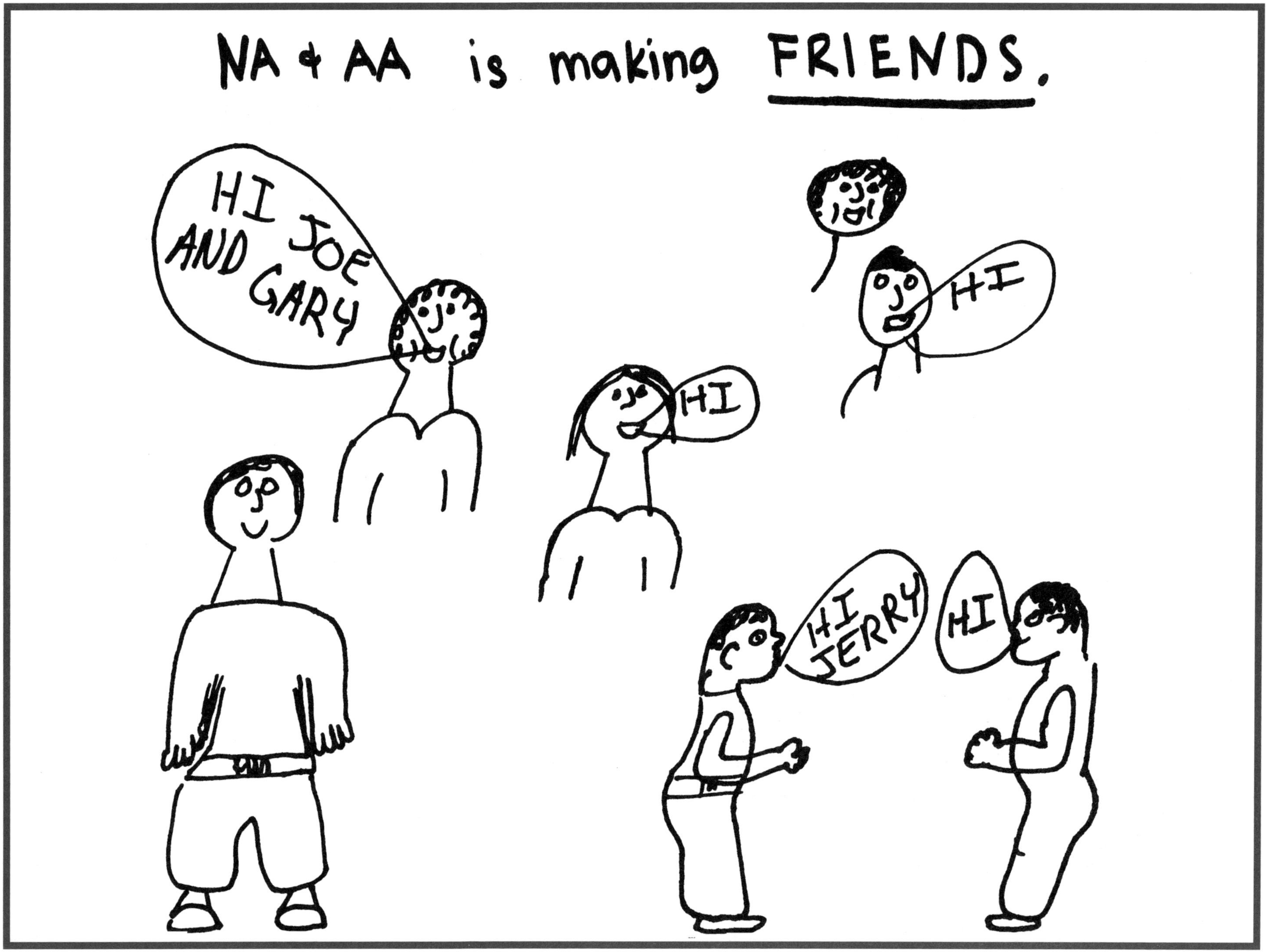
NA & AA is making FRIENDS.
HI JOE AND GARY
HI
HI
HI JERRY
HI

Does your Mom or Dad go to AA, NA or CA? What do you think happens at those meetings?
Draw a picture about it.

I Love my dad more, now when he stopped drinking.

Show how you feel if your Mom or Dad has stopped drinking or using.

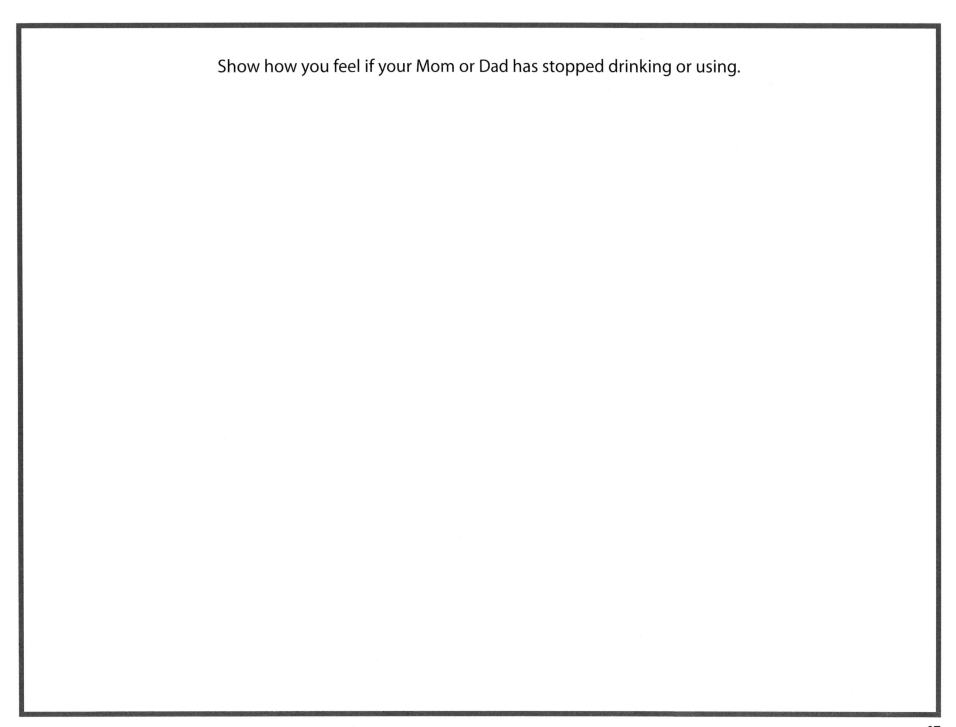

A relapse is when someone drinks for a while then stops, then drinks again. It's like when you have a cold and you think it's gone. Then you go out in the rain and your cold gets worse.

A relapse is when somebody is in the hospital and they get to feel perfectly fine then they get back in.

Has your Mom or Dad ever stopped drinking or using for a long time
and then started to drink or use again? This is called a relapse.
Draw a picture of what happened.

I'm glad my dad doesn't drink any more because he talks with me, & I understand him better, I also like the people at <u>A. A.</u> because they don't just walk away from the kids, we go on a lot of picnics with A. A. and they are more fun than being with a bunch of drunk adults!!

Do you feel a little confused and mixed-up even though your Mom or Dad has stopped drinking or using, like being scared and happy at the same time? If you do, that is normal. You may be very happy your Mom or Dad stopped, but at the same time afraid they may start to drink or use again.

Some Times I still get scared.

Some Times I am Happy

scared

happy

I am glad she is not doing her drugs But sometimes I get worried that she might start again I some Times go up stairs and Sit on my Bed.

People often think that if someone stops drinking or using, everything at home will be fine. This is often true, but not always. You may find that your parents may still argue, blame, or just be unhappy. If your addicted parent has quit their drinking or using but there still seems to be problems at home try not to "give up." It takes time for family problems to work out.

"My dad Feels better and I'm Felling the same way.

If your Mom or Dad has stopped drinking or using, show how things are different now.

Family members often want help so they aren't so confused, scared, or angry. They often ask for help by going to a treatment program or Al-Anon and Alateen meetings. Al-Anon and Alateen meetings are very similar to AA but they are for the family and friends of the addicted person. Al-Anon is for the adults and Alateen is for young people twelve years of age and older.

Now That mom goes to Al-Anon
She smiles more and doesn't
cry So much.

There are a lot of kids who have Alcoholic parents like mine At Alateen I Like getting to know them. It's fun. It's easier to go home.

ALATEEN

Children of all ages can reach out to teachers and counselors at school. It can also help to reach out to other family members, friends, or a friend's parents. There are people who will understand your feelings and concerns. It is okay to ask for help.

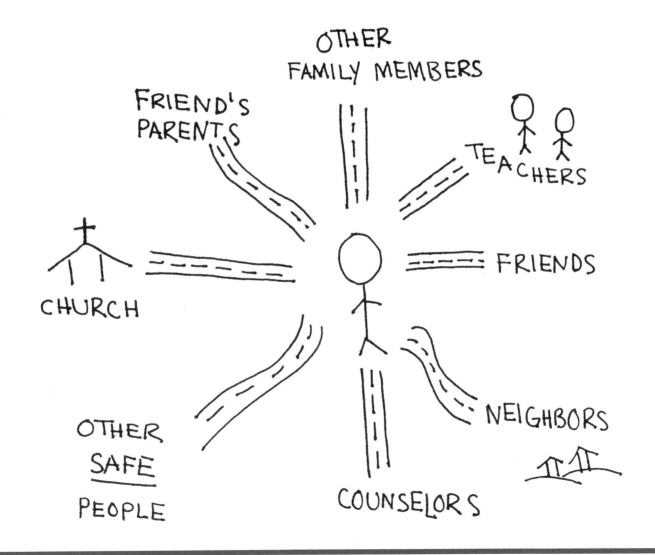

Some things to think about . . .

☆ Alcoholics/addicts can get well.

☆ Alcoholics/addicts only get well when they stop drinking and using. Then the disease of addiction is said to be arrested. This means that the alcoholic/addict will be well as long as he or she doesn't drink or use.

☆ Alcoholics/addicts need to ask other people to help them stop drinking and using. Often they go to a treatment program or to meetings such as AA, CA or NA for help.

☆ Sometimes after they stop drinking or using, they have a relapse. If that happens, they can ask for help again and they can get well again.

☆ Sometimes after our parents stop drinking or using, we have mixed feelings, like being scared and happy at the same time. That is perfectly normal, but it sure helps to talk about our feelings with someone else.

☆ Whether or not the alcoholic/addict stops their drinking or using, the family members and friends can get help.

Remember . . .

If you live in a family affected by addiction, you are not alone. There are many other children, like you, living in homes like yours, who feel just like you do. It is important that you not be ashamed of your feelings or try to push them out of your mind, but that you talk and share your feelings with someone.

Your parents do love you. They just have a hard time letting you know how they really feel because they are sick with the disease of addiction.

It's your turn to draw anything you want.